Sucker Punches

JEFF KILPATRICK

Sucker Punches

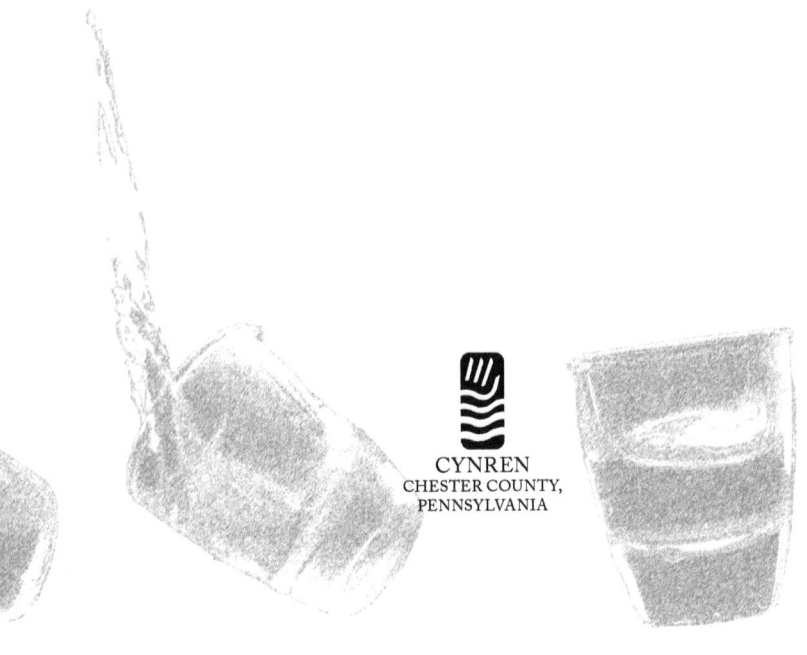

CYNREN
CHESTER COUNTY,
PENNSYLVANIA

PUBLISHED BY CYNREN PRESS
Chester County, Pennsylvania
http://www.cynren.com/

Cynren Press and the Cynren Press logo are registered trademarks of Reodgyfen Inc.

First published 2026

ISBN-13: 978-1-947976-77-1 (pbk)
ISBN-13: 978-1-947976-78-8 (ebk)

Library of Congress Control Number: 2025943691

Content Warning: This book contains themes of Suicide ideation, Alcoholism, Family dysfunction, Relationship trauma.

Cover design by Cynren Press

Contents

Accompaniment

Exposition

"Journey to the Center of the Mind" (The Amboy Dukes)
"Midnight Cruiser" (Steely Dan)

Development

Meditation No. 1 in A Minor: To an Almost Fiancée
"Journey from Mariabronn" (Kansas)

Dispatch from Sector 105
"Fire on High" (Electric Light Orchestra)

A Morning Like Myself
"Wendell Gee" (R.E.M.)
"Country Feedback" (R.E.M.)

Meditation No. 2 in A Minor: Along for the Ride
"Classical Gas" (Mason Williams)

First Movement: Punched
    Gymnopédie No. 1: *Lent et douloureux*

Second Movement: Proving
    Gymnopédie No. 2: *Lent et triste*

Third Movement: Prodigal
    Gymnopédie No. 3: *Lent et grave*

Concerto No. 1: Oaktree

I. Allegretto in Lemon and Cream

Butter, in polos and tees,
in shorts and denim skirts,
wakes me, melts me,
the wedge of salt
jamming the crisper drawer.
To linger is to wilt me,
to postpone me sprouting arms
from each hair on them.
I've got to keep on time
to unlock upstairs windows from the inside,
to step off corn seedlings and fresh baseball,
to change oil, to mow lawns.

II. Adagio in the Colors of Apples

November morning catches its teeth on me.
My breath burns it back,
redeems this paper dollar,
silverplates that one,
stamps the others into gold-angel blood.
Though more pennies than eagles,
they all blaze up,
pretending to be their own children.

III. Funeroso in Earthen Tones

I'm next week's rumor, a whiff
of Oolong, of Cubans,
of the debt that's been made of me.

Every year swallows its tail this way,
but I'd never pawn this key to a mint,
the crypt printed with my face.

I'm closing for winter.

Who cares that I can't afford my vacation?

I'll pay you back when I get there.

Meditation No. 1 in A Minor:
To an Almost Fiancée

after Kansas's "Journey from Mariabronn"

The south wind's fingers dance the open strings
of our love's voice—yes, yours as much as mine.
She snickered at the public pledge I swore you,
taught you how to teach me how to keep
our bedroom window jimmied open, paving
her a boulevard. Each night, through that
she'd slip, sit on the floor, eavesdropping on
your planned-for indecision—six heartbeats
in our first dance, or five? Should each step hire
its own bridesmaid? How would you greet me—
        walking,
sprint yourself on cobwebbed monkey bars?

We shook hands with an unrelenting hike
from our house to a four months' wedding hall;
each minute marched, a hundred clean-trimmed steps.
I should have hand-clamped you, as you would me,
but my arm's more at home around her waist.

You faded to a fade one Monday morning,
tracing ducks' sail toward a pond's far bank.
Appearances convinced you none: "Plum blossoms
sprouting power to swim? Get outta town."
Their bones are tangrams—numbers of their names
hold no effect. Their names are as you read.
Small wonder why I spent that night, and others,
in her bed, or she in mine—or yours.

One morning, over coffee and my gaze
toward *Her*, you waved your ring, a square plus one,
a crown you stutterstepped until the street
undressed us, set us back to walk until
she trout-hooked us with shouts of both our names,
stole me for her blue ribbon.
                              Your six friends
flared Promontory spikes. Out from a maze
of two chromatic trees, we fishtailed, staggered
to the doorstep of forgetting who
left who first—it's all academic now.
Our Christmas gifts were breakups—his and hers,
one size fit both. We kissed our sneak-in girl,
who married me on New Year's.
                              Still, she boasts,
as over tipsy brunch, of tricks by which
you've both seduced a fresh-brought nineteen kid
by willing him or her your families' wealth.

You're drunk with ready fire, will always be.
She's your tall microscope, enough to tell
your scores of thin-sheet notes who keep me played.

Bargain

An open-handed bargain struck us.
I didn't finish telling my suitor Yes,
so Mom can't finish freezing me out.
Where was she, though, when Uncle cheated
on Aunt with her own choir girl,
when he bought her the house next door,

when, despite all that, she blows up
in his face, stubborn heifer as she acts?
Where was she when my cousin
got jealous of Choirgirl, so hotheaded
that she made Uncle watch her lace acid
into her own wedding veil, and forced War—

not just any skirmish, but War itself—
to come so widely between them that one dance
has to last them twenty-six hundred years?
Where was my mother? Watching books
write themselves, while mortals
called us "royalty." My ass we are.

I don't get invited
for winter holidays anymore?
With a family like ours, where's the loss?

Concerto No. 2: For a Blind God

I

Three red-leaf planets
dance with stolen permission,
singing ring-a-rosey
across my lumbar hollow.

Their two neighbors and mine—
opposite first names, same last—
are shoulders lacking strength enough
to shove me off the chains of my ledge.

II

"Find a girlfriend," they said.
"Capital idea," they said.
How could I know
I'd drawn Napoleon's exile?

Even if I could,
she won't let me see her.
She shaved my left eyebrow
and penciled in the star
which orbits her name.

III

Across the street from a beard
no razor can fracture, no hammer shave,
two clocks tell offsetting truths—

an early ocean, and the lockstepped
right now of the five planets.
Both clocks sing, in a unison
they can never jailbreak,
about the dress they wear together,
their pattern the smell
of fresh-dug potatoes.

Hot Peppers for Soup

Fused skulls,
stem-grown with age and experience,
plaster cities' names across their faces
like stickers on suitcases.
With copper or stainless, I lay them open
and sideline promises of tomorrow
into a jar of need,
a kick-start to an overslept morning.
Red and orange are the slower, mellow flame.
Fresh green is too soon
for anything but iron-branded skins.

Whichever the color, they all sink
with the oily grain of a soda can,
greeting him at the bottom of the pot.

He washes into the water, the vegetables,
the garlic, the salt and pepper,
scribbles and scatters all names
across the pleasures of
the tongues he short-circuits.

Dispatch from Sector 105

We're
not possible.
Though we overlap,
we can never collide,
never crack fire into two
cans, crafted from stone and brimming
with breaths our watchers can never catch.

You no more decided telling me my name
was no longer big enough to belong with yours
than decided that I should list and bank, each card
of twenty-one in a full round. We're chained to our inability
to break our chained selves—silent treadmill, an
    eternal parade. No neutron
star will ever unlatch us into a briefcase. We're debris
    sentenced to fifteen
million ambling years, blinded by the elliptical colors of the music
    that wrote us.

accident

after edward and lawrence,
for travis chaney

royalterrible image
its own furnace
of steelglassandrubber

in the
        middleof
                now(here)
with drumbang   hornblow
           and

                            cymbalcrash

deadangels prostrate fall

their libation
of bloodandoilandgasoline
set on sevenfires

while
shadrach   meshach   abednego
        statetrooper   solemn
hire
       testamentbooks
              of
                publicschoolpropagandafilms

swearing   sonsanddisciples
to   sacrilege   and
               (t)reason

Symphony No. 1: Shadows

I. Leaving

We filed into the schoolhouse that morning
at one minute until summer,
only to meet Him—
a gymnastic thief dressed in back-sass green,
standing where Teacher should have stood.

I was the only one brave enough
to ask if Teacher was sick.
The rest saw and knew only Him,
called His name, said hello—
He answered in a language
we didn't know we knew.
He told us He'd paid Teacher
the ransom to redeem the whole Empire.
That's why and when
we watched her stagger away
under twenty guilders for each of us,
down the king's road
toward any coachman's mercies.

He'd pay our parents
the same if we were good, He said.
He'd take care of us if we'd hide
in His mountains until nightfall, He said.
He wouldn't allow anybody to miss us,
or even to think we'd raise any questions
past the already-scheduled end-of-the-year
    picnic.
And so we obeyed, and hid.

At dusk, He left five stars burning,
built us a highway, played it out
on flutes that wore His name.

II. Glimpsing

We'd tramped all night—or had we flown?—
crossing that morning over the border
into a galaxy we've still never heard of,
but we were as fresh as the newly awake.
A mandolin plucked itself off a vine,
a banjo took wing, and we heard ourselves
singing with them, alongside the boulders
that marched into place
to weave His altars and cathedrals.
They sang of goddesses He'd loved,
of princes He'd lost,
of a Devil who walked on a souvenir
from the suburb of a forest,
his hand of doubting silver.

He was right. Our parents didn't miss us.
Every so haphazardly, He'd make us glimpse
our homes. Our parents still ate dinner with us,
tucked us into bed, took us fishing,
kicked cans, rolled stick-hoops.
Though we danced through every motion
of looking the same as when we left,
down to our breaths and blood,
we were breaths with shadows—
make that *a* Shadow. His alone.

III. Reckoning

Shadows' only strength is the setting sun,
the plod of a day
cut free by a going-home whistle
who stretches them twice as wide as tall

until the hour of their deaths.
Our focus, even when we couldn't, rowed
toward an inlet of a sea
with no visible shore;
some of us, toward each other.

Not caring about tune or intent,
we whistled down the sun
one rung, then a second, then two at a time.
Our shadows pledged to us alone.
The sun smiled toward Him—that glib smile
too quickly eager to answer
on the day He paid everyone off—
and abducted Him for a waltz.
Our arms were bows,
our hands strings full of arrows,
our ages the ramparts of churches.
With each mile down the sky,
our loose fire thanked Him
that we once believed,
but since His service wasn't needed anymore,
neither was His life.

Next morning, the sun rose—alone.
Of Himself and His legend-songs, not a quaver.

IV. Returning

The sea held us one final grace, mapped
the opposite shore and our town on it.
Our return voyage is slower,
slower,
as His world refuses to crumble from off our
    bones.

He's returned, as alive
as He'd ever been or will be.

He sneaks in through our children's bedroom
   windows
and pays off teachers while He pipes again
His one tune. His prayer, His chant—
our children's season to follow Him,
to take their turn as shadows,
more His than ours.

We even taught them His address:

"Second star to the Right,
and straight on 'til Morning."

Pinball

My wife knows, but is only jealous by numbers,
of how you wait in the corner,
back to the wall,
for anyone who's enough to light you up.
She watches me lean in to you,
watches me push all your right buttons,
flip you, roll you, spin you,
while I try to guess what number
you're thinking, if you're thinking,
or better, to rename you
into a house on yourself.
I can last longer
on five dollars who care
than on twenty who pretend to.
Otherwise, no one says much.
The girl at the counter nods knowingly,
sells me another roll of quarters.
My wife watches and shrugs,
tells me she'll be all right
as long as I don't spend
all night with you.
Three guys and a woman, whose dates
see them with you, me with you,
ask when I'll let them take their turn
to brush *their* dates off.

Falling

Hamilton County, Nebraska
June 30, 2003

We're twice too light to die—yet. In our final
slipping minutes, a quarter mile for each,
our faces bend by one degree or half,
colliding with rewritten names. Sparks reach
for feet, but find in us no common ground.
We're secondary colors calling late
as always, for our shifts on wavelengths, maps,
and plodding clocks made heavy as we wait
by one too many of the clothes we built
from us, wore us since lunchtime—must you stand
on my lapel?
                    We wilt, fold down to tears
enough to fill a farmer's grateful hand.

An hour from now, we'll dust off, dry out, rise
and work to fall again from our own eyes.

Her Last Day

It's Thursday—perfect for a Sunday drive
contending for Speed Limit of the Year,
except for my appointment with the wife.
She's carsick in the calm, reels in the breeze,
and Alki crosswinds aren't a breath to hold.

Her skin's a poker face with matching winking
hand who never spoke of falling sick,
this weaving through her wedding gown four
    months
ago in plans unplanned, yet none of mine.

She told the date how best to save itself
at courthouse, college quad, the rail depot,
in monuments
              to worlds unfair
                            for twenty-two
years distant, but emblazoned on
a newsreel, or a textbook's byword page.

At twenty 'til eleven, I drove north
from Thurston. Half an hour's slow drift 'til she
threw both our doors aside, screamed out, "I'm
    done!
I'll drown myself before I live another
battered, stumbling day.
                 Ten summers out,
my rubbled reef will stand, my peace will hold
for your next bride to sign a fresh tired cross.
I won't need alimony—just the dog."

The only sound today to mark her time
are new wife, and the old one's "Told ya so."

Still . . . couldn't she have left the dog?

Heavyweights

I didn't
bring any confidence at all
today, any hope to win
this game. Better
for me
to abandon form

and structure—but every time I do, I become the
　　form
that types itself out and scrapes skies. Even
　　swept-up, dusty ideas didn't
have courtesy enough to ask advice from me,
as indeed they never do. All
their striving is to pass off as flowing better,
sounding tighter than they did half a minute
　　earlier. That's their definition of Win.

On that, we'll have to agree to disagree. I'm not looking to
　　win
a sweepstakes or anything. I'm only asking this
　　form
to explain specifically how best I should fill it out.
　　It knows itself better
than I do, has for centuries. It didn't
ask much. Only all
of me,

my banjo-string patience, my straw-clutch to
　　seal words into their correct envelopes. It
　　doesn't need me.
I need it to remind me that one opportune word or
　　thought does not a win

make. The mistake was mine. All
my success lies in this form
as we study each other—but my progress didn't
heal itself. It's reliable in its chronic shortfall at
    any notions of better

performance or of self-understanding. "You'll
    prove better
after time and practice," it whispered—quit
    insulting me
and what's left of my intelligence. It—or should I
    say, You—didn't
approach even the shadow of a win
on your own. That was the arrogant perseverance
    of your assumed abilities. Form
one line—no need for thirty-nine, ya
    victory-lappin' prick. One's all

it takes to dial in to a parade, all
the clay sufficient to summon into existence a
    world inherently better,
where poems can write themselves without
    raising the trouble you do. "Void and
    without form"—
fine start for a world, I'm led to believe. Just don't ask me
for any more help—you've punched me out.
    How's it pretend to feel to pretend to win
by the split breath of a hesitant thought or the
    framing of a knockout word? Didn't

you see—or could you?—that I didn't let you or
    your stinkin' form
win the better
of me after all?

The Three-Square Cathedral

Her name, too tall for casual chat, commands

we cast aside our shoes. Eight centuries
and longer—though she wrenches different frames
from all her pilgrims, her bones spell the name
that paints a landscape for each star, yet sees

as sharply as she's told, not one inch more.
Her platform shoulders, worn too giant-thin
my life until my life ago, still bear
beneath your weight, her own, and mine. Before
she learned to twist in spoken hands, she'd been,
still is, a dancer's solo at a fair,
programmed profession sketched upon her door—
"I'm always free to teach." Come on, go in.
She'll stay parked, yet she'll drive us everywhere.

Painted Weddings: A Summer Suite

I

Mosquitoes are renowned for
their generosity toward me.

Their hands in summer's
wings, lonely only for

me, their superhero signal,
head of their class

in crowds of fifty
or even of one,

press New Testament close,
Braille me with histamine.

II

My brushes, hard enough
to rate on scales,

should know far better
than their "little here,

more there, who'll notice?"
approach that, too often,

paints the fresh drawing
of my own blood.

III

Summer means getting married;
states are no different.

I'm their invitation, torn
open, delivered to the

dorsal ulnar axis of
my left wrist. Time

decides itself by turns.
Sideways, ten to five;

straight up, straight seven.
Three signs are also

invited, their seating chart
a fulcrum of Indecision.

Massachusetts is marrying Hawai'i,
hired Aries to officiate.

IV

Hamal balances, footless as
the Charles spanning Maui.

Sheratan drapes the Cape
across Hilo's sunrise shoulders.

41, hand over Pittsfield.
Raise your full Punchbowl—

it was, huh?
                    Yep.
Our dancer drank all,

dressed as a lie.
Hour hand, feet heavy

as his neighbor's head,
a grappler's hook tattooed

forward and back across
late October sun's anchor,

stinging away from the
face on his freckle.

V

Parties don't wake, clean
after their morning selves.

They need to molt,
melt into brown dwarfs

planed into the mundane
topography of whole skin,

the offices of white-coated
surgeons playing cat's cradle—

what? The painters, back,
whining about too long

missing my company? My
brushes stand ready, high

scent on crimson alert.
Fang marks brand me

with twin brothers' monogram,
my own brother's monogram.

Will I never learn?

A Morning Like Myself

with respect and gratitude to César Vallejo and Donald Justice

I will die in Tulsa, Oklahoma,
on a morning like myself—
indistinguishable from, interchangeable with
a hundred like it in any direction,
a morning to hurry past me on the steps of work,
eye contact scratched off its to-do list.

It will most likely be a Tuesday.
No one ever suspects Tuesday.
It's the middle eight, neither a hook nor a coda.
It's my hand lifting a bear claw to my mouth,
only to change its mind half an inch short
and totter to the table, my arteries on permanent strike.
It's my coffee, lacking brains
or guts enough to call 911,
waiting for Nameless to succeed my job,
for Faceless to assume my lease,
but Tulsa's its own world—
it'll dust off and pick up.

The buses will still have to run;
teachers, to teach;
the phone company, to send bills;
the convenience store half a block down,
to waste people's money
on kosher beef dogs and spicy mini tacos.

Jeff Kilpatrick is dead. No, wait—
he's not so much *dead* as "wasn't,
then was, now won't be ever again."

God, of course, will hear all this,
will exhale through clenched teeth,
an exasperated locomotive
exhausted from forty years' overwork.
Of all eight billion of us,
how dare I be the audacity that scribbles
his Breaking News for the day?
He's already weighed me, Tulsa,
and Tuesdays against the heat-dying sun,
shuffled us into his cabinet of irrelevance.
That sun's last words will be my name.

"Oh, him? He was a moment," God'll say.
"I took a breath, didn't see him—
he'd be a memory, except he isn't.
I do miss convenience stores, though.
Whose arm's a God gotta twist around here
to score some kosher beef dogs
and spicy mini tacos?"

Symphony No. 2:
A Field Guide to Poems and Their Habits
or more simply,
Field Guide

I

Poems are sentient beings.
We prowl for each
other, wandering like Capulet's
backward clown. When we
draw in, caught, they
pitch watch-watching camp on
a lawn of ideas—
but want written immediately,
instead of being assigned
an outlandish Mersenne while
my DMV clerk drones:
"Now serving—Number 1."

II

Poems, when forced to
wait, turn toddler stubborn,
play Hide and Seek,
draft me for It.
They're tornadoes the colors
of bruises, their roundabout
Hellos the fire that
stokes them into themselves.

I ransack my home
to find them, only

to discover how they
don't prefer to arrive.

|||

Poems don't hide, catlike,
in boxes. They left
me traceless, but only
after I obliterated two
boxes of Star Crunch,
one of Swiss Rolls,
a dozen Krispy Kremes,
a Crave Case of
thirty White Castle sliders,
and one box of
Frosted Flakes. (I ate
in handfuls, like popcorn.
Milk is way overrated.)

Poems don't hang heavy
in sacks. Just ask
the oversized bags of
Sweet Chili Doritos, of
maple bourbon beef jerky,
or of Hershey's Miniatures.
I plowed through each
in under five minutes,
but no poems peeked
from under the bottom.

Poems don't tuck neatly
into cans. The garbage
testifies against us both,
brimming with the bones
of a spent case

of Chef Boyardee lasagna
and four tall boys
of honey mustard Pringles.

Poems don't drink beer.
Last one I drank
kept me awake until
noon-thirty on a Sunday.
I set their place
at a breakfast table,
but they sputtered out
with my brewery breath
in traffic they created
expressly for bogging down,
too bashful to tell
me they'd run late.

Poems don't saunter on
coffee breezes. I get
forty minutes per gallon,
but poems are my
luck—sparse as Gobi.
Nothing else to do
but look for them
these three sleepless days.

Poems don't huddle together
like cooked noodles. They
used to enjoy Sichuan
            pork ramen alongside me,
but turn their noses
now, leaving with me
the responsibility to inhale
two pints. (If you
need me, you'll know
where to find me.)

Poems' hobby involves the
art of crafting slips,
unattended, across heavy streets.
They know I can
only wish them back,
not chase them far.
Crossing, I get winded
from the weight of
my lower left leg,
twin to Popeye's forearm.
Spinach can't solve that.

IV

Poems can't play hooky
forever. They get bored,
sneak up behind me,
tap my shoulder. I
need only outrun them,
clever enough of hand
to sit them down,
pry voices from silence.

Poems don't hide where
they don't hide, they
don't travel how they
don't travel, aren't packaged
how they aren't packaged.

Poems gotta be around
somewhere—but I refuse
to hunt their scent
of packs of twenty.
(Smokin's bad for ya.)

July

Iowa drowns in sunshine.
The green crutches, man-tall,
assigned to walk this state forward
turn their coats to a fire blanket thick enough
to wring a square mile and a quarter
into a day's ration for each
of three million acolytes.

There's no cure. Only two remissions:
the combine's appointment with October,
and the notes that write us,
bear us up under our own weight.

All three of our names are true,
but only two have manners enough
for one to piggyback another in a glass cage,
to pencil our blueprint on sidewalks of plastic.
Of our nine bones, you'll see only our smile.

We're a corset on a wasp,
trading weight as we slim down
to a snap in half,
a fingerprint on a blank face.

We're no live fire, but
without us, you wouldn't be, either.

Meditation No. 2 in A Minor:
Along for the Ride

after James Dickey's "Cherrylog Road"
and Mason Williams's "Classical Gas"

The moon and I aren't speaking to each other tonight.
An hour ago, after I told her I was capable
of keeping my own schedule, she left me
to find my own way to morning,
lit by a single land-lamp
too cold to bend silver to its knees,
but sharp enough to joust me with my brothers,
the steel salmon coming home, as I am,
to our stone-painted front porch at the address
of tan x = arcsin x.

Survival hides in hugging the highway's curves
more tightly than any woman
would ever let me do for her.
My orchestra of twelve chariots walks faster
on two feet than I can run on twenty,
over a ladder of fire
which cracks each mile open like green pecans
in waltzes and brass-running elevens

until the sun's front half step,
where she holds her hand out for shaking.
Nothing minor, only major.

Designated Walker:
Arpeggiated Canon No. 1
for Cello in C Major

after Procol Harum's "A Whiter Shade of Pale"

We didn't do *any*thing.
The skipping, the turning,
the vanishing act you
foisted on the tray
of pitchered lager meant
for the whole table—
every ounce of antic,
no signature but yours.

Your girlfriend's facial expressions
ran cold over hot
toward centuries of scandal,
but at least her
porch light's on. She
pretends to be home.

You'd fallen asleep across
a stratus cloud, as
you do every night—
and I, as I
do every night, slung
you across my shoulders
like an ox yoke,
treadmilling a highway sculpted
of polished white brick,
arriving home by a

third at each rise.
I shrugged you into
bed, your snore too
rude to break stride.

We'll be back, same
time tomorrow. You'll blast
yourself, and I'll saunter
us home, the way
friends do—not like
anyone else is gonna.

"Sleepers, awake" . . . I wish.

Symphony No. 3: November

I

My clock radio never remembers its manners.
Just because it's giddy about
waking up at six o'clock,
it thinks I have to be also.
It thinks it can send
"the best mix and variety of the '80s!"
to reach into my eyes, stand
on their wall, flick their switch,
when I'd rather still meditate
on a title and a first line
soon old enough to collect Social Security.

The radio knows, but is too greedy to care.
If I don't work, neither of us eats.
That's why it's so eager to roust me out.

II

It's one degree below dark
and will be for another hour,
now that the sun has renewed
its annual subscription to postponement—
but the streetlight on the opposite corner
is also radio rude. It's clowned all night
in a crystallized grin,
lips sewn to my window,
letters from two and three dimensions
written in base-36, flurried haze

not worth the name, soon to fold
into twenty minutes of light drenching mist.

III

I mope to the kitchen, set the coffee on,
stutter to the bathroom,
let the water shake me loose
from smelling like I've been slept in.
I finish up, open a package of brooms
with plastic finger-length handles
and five bristles carved sharp as fire.

New sweeps clean each time,
and I'm the bleeding floor to prove it,
to spruce it with a two-ply paper mop.

IV

Coffee, creamed and sugared,
hair still damp—this business is a pleasure.

I plug in my black Teflon canvas,
stripe it with my pledge of allegiance
to salt, fat, and deliciousness.
I award it two gold stars.
Would Definitely Recommend.

Once the flag folds onto my plate,
I mix milk into a bowl of supernova dust,
roast it on the night sky until it melts
like a fever dream of Mercury's moons.
I claim this land
in the name of butter and syrup!

Eat, clean up, get dressed
for the job I've got,
not the police visit I don't want.

This border town will either sting me
or shoot me through, but it's polite enough
to tell me where I stand—
at a chilly bus stop, instead
of rolled over in bed,
instead of warm, too out of it
to be less than happy,
or to be made blaringly aware that
my clock radio never remembers its manners.

Common Languages

after Beethoven's Piano Sonata No. 1
in F Minor, and its being featured in the
Peanuts comic strip for December 16, 1957

Though I walk with
my people's dance, my
home's among a tribe
whose staccati I can't
craft, legati all distant
to my tongue's ability
to float like scalpels
or glide like chisels,
to carve inflected bones
into chances of meaning.

We read together, as if
it were a litany,
the reverse aging of
the late afternoon's hair—
lead matte dissolving to
young men's visible invisibility,
time my body never
chooses to take patiently:
native fluency in hunger.

Among my chiefless tribe
of neighbors, a shaman
sings down robins, sparrows,
and a snarling stomach
who's forgotten to care
about words twisting to
chase their own tails,

but not to remain
survivably curious.
                    I follow
myself and this strange
speech that isn't, to
a doorstep that dives
me headlong into comfort
of ready dinner, thumbing
our noses at December's
chill mist—if dinner
or I had thumbs.

Scrub Brush

My morning laundry can't rent
patience for its current inheritance
of two days' sleeping time
sold by encroaching, neighboring trees.
They're all fingerlings, only different
by how many fingers thick.

Human blood's due to serve
its own number this afternoon,
to strike a flowing iron
not fit to be shirt-worn.

To disguise myself more speedily
clean, to dry backyard paths
still damp from January's frost,
I have to carve dents
while I can still count
vagabond hours on hands only.

With each minted minute of
overconfident sunlight, I work at
a deeper cross-purpose to myself,
in shade I must trade
for steel teeth of ingratitude.

My saw can afford, where
I cannot, to whine apologies
to cardinals, goldfinches, cedar waxwings.
I hold them no sympathy,
having spent it all on
knowing where their unfelled nests,
perches, and shelters built themselves.

They're too carefree, safe, happy,
to incline toward pecking stale
meat off a crass sandwich
from a tired fraternity joke.

"Better, tastier luck next year,"
I mumble, a vain consolation
to preempted salads and cakes,
to walnuts the color, softness,
and deliciousness of tennis balls.
The cherries, first red then
black alongside their dinner guests,
grapes laminated in Jackson grey,
don't care that they can't
decide between matte and gloss,
or that they weigh five
to the errant ounce, stand
eighty percent seed by volume.
I've spoken them their peace:
pick handfuls clean, fill water
in pie pan, soak, macerate,
ferment, filter, get toasted—bliss.

Three days' weathering, dry seasoning,
drip revenge from my victims'
fingers. They sweat out tearooms,
while I and my T-shirt
are palates' palettes of desecration—
onions, malt vinegar, chili powder.

My neighbor emeritus, having moved
to Colorado year before last,
crammed his seat cushions full
of indifference toward my pulling
sticks full of hands by
ankles of the abandoned feet
where new legs print leaflets
of once and future names.

His yard's tended by familiar
comfort of its own overgrowth,
weighing unheavily on Someone Else
to happen along, kick-start bonfires
with counterfeit snows who've sold
my clothes on all days
in any sun they'll wear.

Symphony No. 4 in C Minor:
A Suite for Theaters

Illinois, during the Bill Clinton administration
fiction, loosely inspired by true events
after Franz Schubert's Piano Trio No. 2 in E-flat Major, second
movement, and its prominent role in Stanley Kubrick's *Barry Lyndon*

I

Do can't be made indefinitely. Repairs
and inspections will never know how
to carve time enough to learn
to pay for themselves.
      Their friends,
any time new wastes of money
saunter across the grainfields of Illinois,
flounce over traffic in dime-store rainbows
the colors of glass diamond eyes,
brass paint in admission ticket plastic,
slip loose like wallboard panel fragments,
fall short like wiring who should
have resigned alongside John Foster Dulles.

The vaudeville house downtown will testify
to that life, before the interstates
and the drive-ins curtailed its breath.
Its memory camps behind the alley
of the downtown block not shuttered
until Dallas, or demolished until Sadat.

Eight years from now, our Methodist
college, who graciously named this town,

will jockey, jostle with the theater
for heating grate privileges in minds
old enough to remember—or care.
Enrollments' feet have skidded these last
two years, wearing faces of rockslides
of endowment papers forever drawn blank.

II

We're no couple, you and I,
just a guy and a girl,
friends on a bored November Saturday,
a week too early to chase
ourselves into the embrace of gluttony,
but on perfect time to steal
two adjacent seats for this afternoon's
historical society presentation on the centennial
of both institutions, our beloved derelicts.

Sprays of lilacs from McKinnon's shop,
refreshments catered from Subway, generously
    financed
by a bank branched here, but
homed in the pastureland of Chicago—
the historical society and its roommates
are vultures too desperately enjoying hands
of bridge, dealing expired luck across
the bricked-up bones of the theater,
as they will over the college
once our synod defaults the mortgages,
reissues the wildflowers' and native prairie
grasses' licenses to rebuild, rebuy Eden.
(Condos? In this town? Keep dreamin'.)

III

The lightless midday moon's full enough
of herself to forge her nest,

a chin rest for a perfect square.
One lower, she's a perfect cube,
rolling us out of our century,
our jeans and tees, into skins
worn new under memory of houselights.

I'm December in gray Norfolk tweed.
You're my sunny blue Gibson Girl,
a meadow brimming with minor keys.

"Ladies Will Kindly Remove Their Hats."

You have, but your egret feather
stretches onto tiptoe, his share claimed
for the watching.
                    How's that, then?
Improper, you protest, that our fingertips
introduce themselves so darkly, with your
chaperone forgotten on Aunt's parlor's coatrack?
We've a hundred chaperones seated, scattered
across this room, glad to serve
such a turn and without pay.

Our eyes are polite, trained screenward.
Our hands are imps, thread close
as brownstone blocks where your cheek
and my shoulder play hopscotch, skip
rope to echoes of *Eastside, Westside,*
silent and sparse in sepia frames.

IV

The lights ease higher by turns.
The docent thanks us for coming—
"Enjoy the rest of your afternoon!"

Our morning clothes grow back, but
our hands stand reluctant to meander

home from their fond darkness, even
over dinner and settling comfortably into
our dorms for the unhurried evening.

We're not the theater, the college.
They fell, or will. We rose
only for one afternoon, but not
so brusquely as to snicker over
a faintly playful wish like mine:
"Someday, we'll tell our daughters' daughters
we weren't a couple, yet were."

Our voices share the tremor of
our only kiss.

     "We sure will.
I'll tell mine. Go, have fun.
Run the happy risk of yours."

Rude

On a morning when I
could only breathe by yawning,

when five hundred milligrams of pure caffeine
couldn't turn my synapses' ignition key
far enough over to crowbar me out of bed
to the pens and notebooks
on the arm's-reach nightstand,

on that exact make and model of day,
this poem disrupted me.

It cut a careen
past the drive-through line,
double-parked sideways,
somersaulted like a bowling ball
out the passenger side door,
"accidentally" knocked over
my "Please Wait To Be Seated" sign,
and, from two rooms over, woke my wife
by swiping the piece of cake
I'd meant to hold for her breakfast.
It cracked open the plastic clamshell
and saved a seat for the noise
it only ever makes
at three in the morning.

This poem gobbled the cake,
slurped away four ideas flying standby,
then leapt in hard-soled, muddy boots
off the kitchen table.

This poem is a print
that won't mop off the floor.
It laughs with and at
me and itself,
dares me to read it—
a bill for "services rendered."

Postage due and certified,
with me between paychecks—natch.

Song of the Chef's Knife

An exhalation of rain
spattered patiently across the lie
of my hard face,
burnished to tell your soft one.

The tint of Halloween
across my baby picture
borrowed away your trust in me
to break your bread—or you.

I need back into keen trim.
Bathe me in a letter
no eyes can read,
in the gibberish under your fingers

until you stand me tall
in Eau de Sauerkraut
up to the grip of my neck.
Whisk me in saltless tears,

wand me as though you're wielding me,
then tell me I'm ready.
Tell the onions, the celery, and the carrots
today just resigned from being their day.

Cleaning Up After the Party

The westbound breeze comes groping for its
    misplaced
feet again, sprawled on a roof of wistful
leaf stems, bargain-basement rain in shades
of Morse code—but from seekless hides, no shoes
come volunteering out to play.

                              Dawn fades,
stands seven-fifteen tall, sings down its blues,
pinks, Easter-egg-dye yellow, slender green.

The sun, still doubled over from last night,
groans, punch-drunk, cleans smudged handprints
    off its screens
with inch-wide dots of Sharpie ink scorched
    bright
by isopropyl kisses, dusts away
the brink of Mars-shaped blemish from the eyes
of his port beam, disguises all as Day:

"Too busy. Can't talk now. I'm late to rise."

Almond Bread

after Jefferson Airplane's "White Rabbit"
and Tommy James and the Shondells'
"Crystal Blue Persuasion"

I'm a crumb, a slice,
an uncarved loaf, the aroma
of the sun's leather belt
so tight it prints him

into a hernia, aimed backward
from his right shoulder blade.
I'm a mile of film
escaped to surf dragon's tails.

¿Matándome con fuego? Buena suerte.
Fire's my hometown of stones
grinding my bones to rise
and walk into your plate.

Obey me, like Alice did.
Watch me sprout, Cheshire cross-eyed,
a bowsprit waving to myself,
tattooed with my own lifespan.

Ourselves: An Introduction

We're another night—spent
spending each other bankrupt,

scratch-off tickets rebuying themselves
into cracked cookie misfortunes.

We're shadows of fingertips,
a waltz on precipices

of my whipcrack wrist
over strings and fretboards

who've never forgiven me,
nor I them, that

we ever learned how
to play each other.

We're an open palm
of frozen clocks, fingers

jointed with indictments reassuring
me with doubts, each

as guilty of me
as I of them.

We're drivers whose stations
dial in to us

on each morning's commute,
strand our Off button

in a rest stop
who stops our rest

until we're scattered awake

into another night—spent.

Sick Day No. 1:
The Importance of Never Letting
a Crisis Go to Waste

Deaf shoulders and cold ears
couldn't turn down the chill
of a piccolo breeze's vibrato.

I'm now saddled to my
bucking bronchi, glued to them
with the insolence of congestion,

of a camel threading teeth
of my coughing needle, kneading
my head into stubborn bread.

The road back to myself
pours strata of blankets over
me, keeps me down better

than the lasagna or cake
they see in their mirror,
but who'd choke me on

the suspicion or taste of
themselves, dividing empty by empty.
I balance a week's worth

of oranges on my fingernails,
fool them down the trapdoor
of recovery, my right cup

of tea.
        Because my eyes
rose into fire written to
build me from the inside,

set me on me,
                I'm
a cure, sitting beside myself.

Concerto No. 3: Magnificent Mile

after Mike Oldfield's "Tubular Bells," Part 1,
George Enescu's Sonata for Cello and Piano in F Minor,
and Mark Mothersbaugh's "111 Archer Avenue"
for Craig and Wendy Ward

I.   Down to the Street

We're dressed in a trip
across our ice water feet,

waiting beside a door hinged
with scales of fifteen stones,

a finger wave, a pendulum
for the kindness of Lightning.

In sixty-two seconds, he'll bolt
down a dominant staircase, play

Marco Polo, rack himself clean,
six ball, upper right corner

pocket, shatter himself in a
breeze five tones too sharp.

II.   Out in the Street

Snowplow sirens on concrete rocks
hum drowsy static, next blocks.

Red kettles in sleighbell keys
busk for compassion no wind

can afford them. Baseball sends
postcards from sunny thumbed noses.

Green tire swings, rivers' names,
splinter us into sixteenth notes,

pop us like preemptive corks
across hoods, windshields, and crosswalks.

III. Home from the Street

The cold clings us to
each other like summer mud

on Arizona Territory boots, lonely
for company warm enough to

erase us. Comfort compels us
back, as for jury duty,

as though we'd forgotten our
keys and wallet on the

table in the front hallway.

Our hands crush ourselves into

nine voices, full month's sentence,
tall houses buttoned to the

city's lapel.
                    The wind wakes,
plants petrichor in our memory,

keeps us a breakfast date
at Saint Joseph's opposite table.

Concerto No. 4: Midwestern Midspring

I

In a tree
off the sidewalk,
maple leaves thicken
like coming attractions
of syrup.

Nine species of
songbirds wear branches
thick as Halloween
masks, conspire for
joy at

mornings which hide
them so deeply
we can't read
their songs, write
their names.

II

On a sidewalk
off the tree,
café patrons scatter
sun into bagels
and coffee

creamed and sugared
with shorter shirts,
skirts, and shorts

so low our
jackets melt

in twelve Celsius
degrees, our bravado
skin bared, chilling
with us, drumming
its fingers

to crossed wires
in inhuman breaths,
their men dressed
in flags, their women
in homebuilding.

III

In each other
off each other,
we're microscopes, slides
of sliced culture,
each straining

out our common
static, tuned in—
mundane on mundane,
survival on survival,
nested inside

wanting, but unable
to tell murmur
from murmur, faces
from faces, without
a program.

I'm

I'm the patience of water,
rain so faint its claw
weighs its needed time, scores
my slender shoulders of paper
through a centimeter of roof.

I'm snow beads drawn to
fall onto my inbox, corner
scattered, stacked with drafts shaky
enough to turn Jenga granite.

I'm a car sent from
the factory thirteen years late,
rusty chassis and moldy upholstery.

I'm a defaulted promissory note,
interest accrued, redeemed only when

I'm writing these ideas out.

Concerto No. 5:
Water Under the Bridge

after Robert Browning's "How They Brought the
Good News from Ghent to Aix" and Led Zeppelin's
"No Quarter"

I

Below and behind anklebones
in need of rewriting,
mistranslated centuries of oak
armorless against pitched strikes
from me or from
a succession of steel,
I trudge my bed—
unfitted, jagged top sheets
thick as innuendo, as
colors of scrambled theorems
in prime powers, discontinuous
at points of origin.

II

Fifty paces due north,
behind the walls of
a keep at the
intersection of three languages,
the good news (whose
name hasn't unmasked itself
since it charged out)
admires the grateful breaths
of its best self,

delivered to itself: having
served its faithful turn
that apprehensive morning of
late May's farm fields.
It's reprieved from marching
in worthy hammers, scratching
hillocks of worn-out blankets
off a cleared road
like a trinket ticket,
playable only until it
unravels, my name's finger
sketching itself onto itself.

III

I'm vines of triatomic
dust, predator's patience, teaching
steel to read maps,
to tighten sheets into
clean stretches of powers
in coded binary, coups
against these moldering woods
and five rusty centuries.

The good news is,
the good news can
now gallop in coaches,
sideline me with hands
wide as new highways
where I can't hitch
myself to any disappointment
that the news left.

I'll stay in bed
and tread my mill.

I don't have better
to go or do.

Compression No. 1:
Don't Follow My Hand

Don't follow my hand.
It can't trust itself
to sculpt itself into a proper poem. Don't trust
your eyes to follow ideas onto silver plates they
    can't hand

themselves on. A hand by itself can't
thread breezes of imagination through word
    windows they don't follow, or make them trust
enough to trust my hand to follow
itself off a scrap heap into a whole. I don't—
    more to the point, can't—

un-telegraph their punches, can't trust
    second-guessing them, and I don't
pick patience like strawberries. My hand, left to
    itself, will follow
where "follow" can't find its way home from itself
while I trust my writing hand to know what I don't.

Don't let this poem mislead you or itself. It knows
    enough not to follow
or to trust anywhere it can't lead my hand.

Weapons of Choice

to the memories of Hazel Cagle and Carolyn LaBounty Goats
November 1983

Until mid-morning of my third-grade year,
I never held a pen as much as wielded,
scratched right answers over smudgy pin-striped
snow, a dagger's faithful sinker pitch.

My teachers passed their plates of patience toward
the tricorn rubber prism coiled across
each pencil's shoulders, elbowing my grasp
off my path into its, narrow from wide.

By Christmas lunch, my javelins slenderized
to chopsticks, scalpels, darts, to sharper whittled
points each word sculpts from its brute finesse.

Four decades since my grip's gait shook off
   "stab"
for shoes named "paint" in targets ripe to plant
what you've read here.
                I'm no less weaponeer.

Sick Day No. 2:
Why Caffeine Isn't Recreational
but Medicinal

My blood missed my blood today.
The first is lonely, because the second
aimed against her aim.
My slow blankets bound me swiftly,
folded me over and in
like eggs and brownie batter
in the same beaten mirror.

My half-life skin cells flake to the floor,
into the eighty-two endgame dance steps
who led my feet into femurs' stubborn concrete heft.
My tongue's a holding pattern sunrise
on an overhumid back road, a taste
as underirrigated as this slice of paper,
shallow as a penknife's rattle
in an unsharpened well.

It took this day of muddying me
into seeing my way clear—
I can't see clearly without my two glasses,
cracked open, poured out.

Because of them,
I don't have health that's good,
but because of them,
I do have health. That's good.

Concerto No. 6:
Sucker Punch

for Coree O'Donnell and Micah Bright

First Movement: Punched

Two jarring slugs of white Payne County lightning
woke me to the cork pop of your kiss:
"We love each other—that's what broke us up."

I've never met a draft so strong as this.

Work-ordered stones heaped tall on gravity,
their saccharine taunt of loitering bouquet,
refused to learn to fold or iron themselves,
to pack where they could hang or tuck away.

They propped their feet; across their shoulders, draped
one well-tired name of "passing in and out
from night to morning."

                Nothing fit so well
on us as getting drunk on every doubt
you'd sober back up soon.

                    Pass me that bowl
of stumbling on your best time to go cold.

Second Movement: Proving

I weighed two shots—the first I kept to sample;
one, detained. The longer-suffering ground

held patient. I G-manned a keg for him,
while Sent Back settled home for one more round.

One hundred forty proof, more distillations
than my years of life—step by slow turn,
the mellowed tones of lying spice I hoped
revealing, never warmed so much as burned.

One afternoon, the barrel held a pint;
next morning stood so fat I couldn't lift.
I sipped, saved one, tossed off the angels' share,
and so again mailed my impatient gift

To Sometime, should his schedule ever find
a breath to test my craft, name it Refined.

Third Movement: Prodigal

I didn't quit that job. The job quit me,
stole fifteen years of given damns to pack.
She slung herself across her shoulder, sauntered
out our drive, watched me not chase her back.

The bottle sheltered one exhausted ounce.
Our names, engraved, had rusted, dripped away.
The only memory kind enough to keep
on time with rent? My journal from that day:

"Sad friends. Great hooch. Three blottos. World's.
        Best. Night."

I huffed the dust aside, choked out my last—
We've finally faded out, but weren't we fun—
you're at the door? Come in! But why's each glass

so topped up? Yeah, my job called, booked a flight.
Stick close, and we'll all drink tomorrow night.

Acknowledgments

In the first chapter of his epistle, Saint James reminds us that "every good and perfect gift is from above" (1:17). I'm just a man, so I won't lay any claim that this is perfect. I am, however, willing to offer it as good, or close to it. *Sucker Punches* represents a return from a fifteen-year exile, and it is my offering of thanks to the God who made me a writer and who created the caffeine which assists me in that. I'll never let you down like that again, Sir.

I thank Cynren Press—more specifically, its wonderful publisher, Holly Thesieres Monteith—for taking a chance on someone without previous journal publication credits or (as of April 2026) an MFA. You have been amazingly kind and patient to a first-time author, and you will always have my heart that way.

To my immediate family—Mom, Dad, John, Andrew, Taylor—I give my thanks for (among so, so much more than noted here) their love and support through these years of my life, and for sharing my happiness when Cynren told me I had the high sign.

Mark Cox, who taught the Poetry Writing workshop in the Department of English at Oklahoma State University in spring 1995, showed me what it is to properly act on being a poet, especially the "every man his own editor, reviser, most stringent critic" aspect. To learn this is to learn what it is to be not just a versifier but closer to a craftsman, an artisan. I am indebted to him—in that respect, *Sucker Punches* is as much his as mine.

I thank the many, many friends I made along the way during my time at OSU from 1993 to 1997, especially those who resided alongside me in Parker Honors Hall, for crossing my path, as I did theirs, and for letting me glimpse their lives and hearts, as they did mine. The years I spent with them were the golden years of my life—

And then there's the platinum years, the diamond, the tanzanite. To my Liz, to whom I was married for twenty-eight years until her passing in October 2025, I offer my eternal thanks for her love, her patience, her forbearance, her goodness of sport at being my guinea pig as I worked through this draft, that revision, the other final product. *This book is for you, honey—you and these mentioned attributes.* Rest well until we meet again.

JEFF KILPATRICK holds a BA in English from Oklahoma State University and one-third of an MA in each of three different fields, English, secondary English education, and statistics, from the University of Nebraska–Lincoln. He lives outside Davenport, Iowa, and has yet to determine whether he drinks caffeine to spark inspiration or claims such inspiration to excuse his considerable caffeine habit.

Stay in the conversation.

We invite you to join Cynren Press's
Margin Notes
—where we share thoughtful essays,
early looks at forthcoming books,
and conversations that extend
beyond the page.

cynren.com/margin-notes

www.ingramcontent.com/pod-product-compliance
Ingram Content Group UK Ltd.
Pitfield, Milton Keynes, MK11 3LW, UK
UKHW042158140526
12486UKWH00004B/192